Fun on the Farm

AT THE ORCHARD

By Bruce Esseltine

Gareth Stevens
PUBLISHING

Please visit our website, www.garethstevens.com. For a free color catalog of all our high-quality books, call toll free 1-800-542-2595 or fax 1-877-542-2596.

Cataloging-in-Publication Data

Names: Esseltine, Bruce.
Title: At the orchard / Bruce Esseltine.
Description: New York : Gareth Stevens Publishing, 2017. | Series: Fun on the farm | Includes index.
Identifiers: ISBN 9781482455281 (pbk.) | ISBN 9781482455304 (library bound) | ISBN 9781482455298 (6 pack)
Subjects: LCSH: Orchards–Juvenile literature. | Fruit-culture–Juvenile literature.
Classification: LCC SB357.2 E87 2017 | DDC 634–dc23

First Edition

Published in 2017 by
Gareth Stevens Publishing
111 East 14th Street, Suite 349
New York, NY 10003

Copyright © 2017 Gareth Stevens Publishing

Editor: Ryan Nagelhout
Designer: Laura Bowen

Photo credits: Cover, p. 1 Oksana Shufrych/Shutterstock.com; p. 5 Monty Rakusen/Cultura/Getty Images; pp. 7, 24 JennaWagner/E+/Getty Images; p. 9 Tim Large/Shutterstock.com; p. 11 (plums) Boida Anatolii/Shutterstock.com; p. 11 (lemons) grafnata/Shutterstock.com; p. 11 (oranges) chanwangrong/Shutterstock.com; p. 11 (peaches) Leena Robinson/Shutterstock.com; p. 13 Alexander Mazurkevich/Shutterstock.com; p. 15 Dmytro Balkhovitin/Shutterstock.com; pp. 17, 24 Fotokostic/Shutterstock.com; pp. 19, 24 Ortodox/Shutterstock.com; p. 21 l i g h t p o e t/Shutterstock.com; p. 23 Thaweewong Vichaiururoj/Shutterstock.com.

Printed in China

CPSIA compliance information: Batch #CW17GS: For further information contact Gareth Stevens, New York, New York at 1-800-542-2595.

Contents

Some farmers
take care of trees.

These trees grow fruit!
This is called
an orchard.

Farmers plant trees
in rows.

These trees grow different fruits.

Many farms grow apple trees.

Most apples are red.
Some are green!

Some trees make
tiny red fruits.
These are cherry trees.

Other trees grow pears.

People pick the fruit
off trees.

They get to eat it!

Words to Know

cherry

orchard

pear

Index